BOOKS BY SEAMUS HEANEY

POETRY
Death of a Naturalist
Door into the Dark
Wintering Out
North
Field Work
Poems 1965–1975
Sweeney Astray: A Version from the Irish
Station Island
The Haw Lantern
Selected Poems 1966–1987
Seeing Things

CRITICISM
Preoccupations
The Government of the Tongue

PLAYS
The Cure at Troy: A Version of Sophocles' Philoctetes

THE CURE AT TROY

A Version of Sophocles' Philoctetes

THE CURE

AT TROY

A VERSION OF

SOPHOCLES'

Philoctetes

SEAMUS HEANEY

The Noonday Press
Farrar, Straus and Giroux
New York

Library of Congress catalog card number: 91-73600

In memory of Robert Fitzgerald
poet and translator
1910–1985

'O look, look in the mirror,
  O look in your distress;
Life remains a blessing
  Although you cannot bless.

O stand, stand at the window
  As the tears scald and start;
You shall love your crooked neighbour
  With your crooked heart.'

W. H. AUDEN

CHARACTERS

ODYSSEUS
NEOPTOLEMUS
PHILOCTETES
CHORUS

Attendants to Neoptolemus, at least three:
CHORUS LEADER
SENTRY
MERCHANT *(in disguise)*

HERCULES *(in person of chorus leader)*

THE CURE AT TROY
*was first performed at the Guildhall, Derry,
on 1 October 1990.
The cast included:*

ODYSSEUS	*Seamus Moran*
NEOPTOLEMUS	*Sean Rocks*
PHILOCTETES	*Des McAleer*
CHORUS	*Veronica Duffy*
	Siobhan Miley
	Zara Turner

Directors	*Stephen Rea and*
	Bob Crowley
Designer	*Bob Crowley*
Lighting designer	*Rory Dempster*
Music	*Donal Lunny*

THE CURE AT TROY

A Version of Sophocles' Philoctetes

A sea shore. Spacious fetch of sea-light. Upstage right (from audience's point of view) rocks piled, cliff-face, grass tufts, stunted bushes. A cave mouth/archway visible up there, with small acting area at that level. A sort of strewn pathway, coming downstage, forking towards acting area. Access to cave mouth possible from this point. Access to second entrance of cave is offstage, right. If a volcano can be suggested in background, all the better; but it should not be overemphasized.

CHORUS discovered, boulder-still, wrapped in shawls. All three in series stir and move, like seabirds stretching and unstiffening. The prologue can be divided among the three voices. By the end of the prologue, CHORUS LEADER has positioned herself where she will speak as HERCULES at the end of the play.

CHORUS

Philoctetes.
            Hercules.
                        Odysseus.
Heroes. Victims. Gods and human beings.
All throwing shapes, every one of them
Convinced he's in the right, all of them glad
To repeat themselves and their every last mistake,
No matter what.

            People so deep into
Their own self-pity, self-pity buoys them up.
People so staunch and true, they're fixated,
Shining with self-regard like polished stones.

1

And their whole life spent admiring themselves
For their own long-suffering.
                              Licking their wounds
And flashing them around like decorations.
I hate it, I always hated it, and I am
A part of it myself.

                    And a part of you,
For my part is the chorus, and the chorus
Is more or less a borderline between
The you and the me and the it of it.

                    Between
The gods' and human beings' sense of things.

And that's the borderline that poetry
Operates on too, always in between
What you would like to happen and what will –
Whether you like it or not.

                    Poetry
Allowed the god to speak. It was the voice
Of reality and justice. The voice of Hercules
That Philoctetes is going to have to hear
When the stone cracks open and the lava flows.
But we'll come to that.
                              For now, remember this:
Every time the crater on Lemnos Island
Starts to erupt, what Philoctetes sees
Is a blaze he started years and years ago
Under Hercules's funeral pyre.

The god's mind lights up his mind every time.

Volcanic effects. Lurid flame-trembles, commotions and
eruptions.

   Then, a gradual, brightened stillness. The CHORUS *are now*
positioned as lookouts attending the entry of ODYSSEUS *and*
NEOPTOLEMUS.

   Enter NEOPTOLEMUS *and* ODYSSEUS.

                    ODYSSEUS
   Yes.
          This is the place.
                         This strand.
   This is Lemnos all right.

                              Not a creature!

   And here we are then, Neoptolemus,
   You and me.
                Greeks with a job to do –
   But neither of us nearly half the man
   Your father was.
                    Achilles had nobility.

                                   Achilles stood
   Head and shoulders above everybody.

   Yes. I left Philoctetes here.

                         Marooned him – but
   Only because I had been ordered to.
   I did it, all the same. I am the one
   That dumped him, him and his cankered foot –
   Or what had been a foot before it rotted
   And ate itself with ulcers.

                         It was awful.
   We couldn't even get peace at the altar
   Without him breaking out in these howling fits,

3

And slabbering and cursing.
                              He was putting us on edge.
He couldn't be stopped.

                    Everybody's nerves were getting raw.

Anyway.
            That was then.
The thing is different now entirely – so
Go canny.
                                        One false move
And everything is wrecked.

Somewhere here he has a sort of den,
An open-ended shelter that gets sun
In the wintertime and in the summer
Has a breeze that cools him.
And down a bit there, over to the left –
Unless the spring's dried up, you should see water.

Go very easy now.
                    Study the lie of the land
And then we'll plan the moves.

I can see the whole thing in my head,
So all you'll need to do is listen
And do the things I tell you.

NEOPTOLEMUS
Odysseus. For sure, sir. This is it.
This cave is the one that you remember.

4

ODYSSEUS

Whereabouts? I can't see any cave.

NEOPTOLEMUS

Up here, above you. But there's no sign of him.

ODYSSEUS

Take care he's not inside there, dozing.

NEOPTOLEMUS

There's a pile of old leaves somebody has slept on.

ODYSSEUS

And is that it? No other signs? That's all?

NEOPTOLEMUS

No: wait. There's a mug or something, very rough,
Hagged out of a log. And bits of kindling.

ODYSSEUS

All his earthly goods.

NEOPTOLEMUS

Aww! Look at this.
Aw! Rotten, rotten stuff. Bandage-rags.
Nothing but old dry pus and dirty clouts.

ODYSSEUS

That's it. That's him:
So he has to be around.
With a foot like his, he'll not be travelling far.
Out scavenging, likely,
Poking for things to eat, or maybe out

Gathering herbs to try to get relief.
Anyway, he's going to be back,

                  And something tells me, soon –
So get your lookout posted. We can take no risks.
I am the marked man here.

                   Of all the Greeks,
I am the one that Philoctetes wants.

NEOPTOLEMUS

This man here's

Exit ATTENDANT.

              a watchman you can trust.
        But you're going to have to tell me more
About these moves you're planning. What's going on?

ODYSSEUS

Neoptolemus. There's a noble streak in you
And you're a strong man.

                Truly your father's son.
But you're going to have to tell me more

              Force isn't going to work.
So, if parts of this brief seem puzzling to you,
Just remember: you're here to serve a cause.

NEOPTOLEMUS

What are the orders?

ODYSSEUS

You're going to have to work out some way, you,
Of getting round Philoctetes with a story.
He'll ask you who you are and where you're from

6

And you'll say, Achilles' son, which will be true.
And that you're on your voyage back from Troy,
Heading home in a rage against the Greeks.
And you can make the rage look natural if you say
You were insulted.
                    You'll tell him
How the Greeks begged and coaxed you to join up
And leave your native place because you –
                              you and only you –
Were the man they absolutely needed.

Troy could not be taken without you.

Well then. You land at Troy. You naturally
Expect to be presented with the arms
Your father bore. You are Achilles' son.
But Odysseus is the man who bears those arms.
Odysseus tricked you. Odysseus this and that!
You can let loose at me for all you're worth.
The worse it is the better you'll please me.
If I am not the lowest of the low
By the time you're finished, the Greek cause is doomed.
For the old story actually is true:
Without you, Troy cannot be taken.

                              We need you.
To commandeer the bow from Philoctetes.

And always remember this:
                      you are the only one
That can approach him. You weren't sworn in
On the first expedition, you didn't sail
Under oath to anybody. Your slate is clean.

7

But if I was challenged, I could not deny
Any of that. And if he recognized me
And had his bow with him, I would be dead.
And you'd be dead for associating with me.
So the trick you're going to have to turn is this:
                              Sweet talk him and relieve him
Of a bow and arrows that are actually miraculous.

But, of course, son, I know what you are like.
I know all this goes against the grain
And you hate it. You're a very honest lad.
But, all the same, even you have to enjoy
Coming out ahead.
                         Do it my way, this once.
All right, you'll be ashamed
                              but that won't last.
And once you're over it,
                         you'll have the whole rest of your life
To be good and true and incorruptible.

I hate hearing you say this
                         and I hate more
The thought of having to do it.
                              It goes against
All I was ever brought up to believe.
It's really low behaviour.
                         Why could we not
Go at him, man to man? If he's so badly lamed
He'd never be a match for two of us.

We're Greeks, so, all right, we do our duty.
I don't think I could bear being called a traitor.

8

But in all honesty I have to say
I'd rather fail and keep my self-respect
Than win by cheating.

ODYSSEUS
Neoptolemus,
As long as you're alive
your father's never going to be dead.
And in my day, I was the same as you.
I'd lift my hand before I'd use my brains.
But experience has taught me: the very people
That go mad at the slightest show of force
Will be eating out of your hand if you take them right
And tell the story so as to suit just them.

NEOPTOLEMUS
Which boils down to a policy of lies.

ODYSSEUS
Arguments wouldn't work, no more than force.

NEOPTOLEMUS
So just how dangerous is this famous bow?

ODYSSEUS
The arrows never miss and always kill.

NEOPTOLEMUS
But if you go at him close in, hand to hand?

ODYSSEUS
Combat is out. We have to use the head here. I've told
    you.

NEOPTOLEMUS

You don't think lying undermines your life?

ODYSSEUS

Not if it will save life, and save the day.

NEOPTOLEMUS

You can look me in the eye and still say that?

ODYSSEUS

Scruples are self-indulgence at this stage.

NEOPTOLEMUS

So what stage is it? Why must he go to Troy?

ODYSSEUS

We need his weapons if we're to take the town.

NEOPTOLEMUS

You said without me Troy would not be taken.

ODYSSEUS

But not without his weapons.
                    Nor the weapons without you.

NEOPTOLEMUS

Well then.
          So be it.
                    The weapons are our target.

ODYSSEUS

And once you have them, you'll have triumphed twice.

NEOPTOLEMUS

In what way twice?
                    Is this more double-talk?

ODYSSEUS

You'll be praised for courage first.
                    Then for farsightedness.

NEOPTOLEMUS

Duplicity! Complicity!
                    All right.
                              I'll do it.

ODYSSEUS

Do you remember everything I told you?

NEOPTOLEMUS

I have said I am going to do it.
                    Trust me.

ODYSSEUS

So. Well. What you do now is wait for him.
I'm going to have to leave in case he sees me.
And I'll take that watchman with me.
                              But one last thing.
If I think you are being held up for what seems
A dangerously long time, I'll send the man back.
He'll be dressed up like a ship's captain, you know,
All innocence and full of sailor-talk,
But you'll be fit to read between the lines
For the message, whatever the message is.
                    Well, if there's nothing else,
I'm away to the ship. It's in your hands now.

Hermes that guides the go-betweens and dealers
Be your protector, and Athene too,
My own best patron.

Exit ODYSSEUS.

CHORUS

What are the likes of us to do?
We're here and we're supposed to help you,
But we're in a maze.
We're strangers and this place is strange.
We're on shifting sand. It is all sea-change.
Clear one minute. Next minute, haze.
But you are blessed with special insight,
So tell us, son.
Give us our instructions.

NEOPTOLEMUS

Be very careful as you go.
Keep on the lookout for the creature,
But watch me too
In case I signal.

CHORUS

We'll do that. Don't you worry, sir.
That's what we are here for.
But what about this wild man on the loose?
Is his head away? Is he dangerous?
Does he live in a den or a house?

NEOPTOLEMUS

His shake-down is up there
In a sort of roofed-in place under the rocks.

12

And where is he?

NEOPTOLEMUS
Out scavenging, somewhere near.
His old gifts as an archer
Stand him in good stead.
But all the same, it's sad.
Him, the master bowman, the great name,
Dragging himself through bushes after game.
Festering inside and out.
Contrary, hard and proud.

CHORUS
It's a pity of him too
Afflicted like that,
Him and that terrible foot.
And not a one to talk to.
Like the last man left alive.
How does the being survive?

Human beings suffer
But not to this extent:
You would wonder if it's meant.
Why him more than another?
What is the sense of it?

Out in the open always,
Behaving like a savage.
Nothing but squeals and laments.
Nothing left but his instincts.
Howling wild like a wolf.

NEOPTOLEMUS

In one way, it does make sense.
It all had to happen – the snake-bite at the shrine.
And everything that happened since.

Fate works in its own time.
                              If he had sailed then
Troy would have fallen too soon.
                              But this is now.

PHILOCTETES *begins to cry out, offstage.*

CHORUS

Quiet. Wheesht!

NEOPTOLEMUS

This is the hour of the bow!

                              Listen to that . . .
He is in awful pain.
                  That squeal
Must be every time he drags his foot.

CHORUS

Watch out. Get ready.

NEOPTOLEMUS
How?

CHORUS

                              Think of your plan.
This is not some shepherd in a book
With his Pan pipes and his shepherd's crook.

14

This is a danger-man.
That shouting's desperate and it's violent.
He sounds provoked.

      He maybe saw the boat.

Enter PHILOCTETES.

      PHILOCTETES
What's this? Who is this here? How did you land?
What brought you to a deserted island?
Tell us who you are and where you come from.
Your clothes look Greek and that warms my heart
But I need to hear your voices.
I know I look like a wild animal
But don't let that scare you.

         Don't treat me
Like an untouchable.

      What I am
Is what I was made into by the traitors.
Do the friendly human thing and speak.

     NEOPTOLEMUS
All right.

    I can tell you this:

        What warms your heart
Warms ours.

    We are Greeks.

     PHILOCTETES
Ohh! Hearing you talk,

       just hearing you
And seeing you –

     you have no idea

15

How much that means.
                              But who was it sent you?
Was it only chance?
                              Or was there purpose to it?
Did a wind blow you off course?
Tell me what happened and who you are.

NEOPTOLEMUS

The whole story is very short and simple.
My home-ground is the island of Scyros
And I am heading for its wave-lashed shores.
My name is Neoptolemus. Achilles was my father.

PHILOCTETES

Then you are one lucky son, and a lucky sailor
To be heading for that home. But where are you coming
    from?

NEOPTOLEMUS

The walls of Troy. We hoisted sail at Troy.

PHILOCTETES

What's that you say? You must have been with us.
Did you not sail with the original Greek force?

NEOPTOLEMUS

Do you mean to say that you sailed with that force?

PHILOCTETES

Och! Och! Och ho!
                              Child, do you not know me?

NEOPTOLEMUS

How could I know a man I never saw?

PHILOCTETES

And you haven't even heard my name . . . ?
Och ho!
          Or heard about the way that I'm afflicted?

NEOPTOLEMUS

Never. I have no notion
                    what all this is about.

PHILOCTETES

Gods curse it!
                    But it's me the gods have cursed.
They've let my name and story be wiped out.
The real offenders have got away with it
And I'm still here, rotting like a leper.
Tell me, son. Achilles was your father.
Did you ever maybe hear him mentioning
A man who had inherited a bow –
The actual bow and arrows that belonged
To Hercules, and that Hercules gave him?
Did you never hear, son, about Philoctetes?
About the snake-bite he got at a shrine
When the first fleet was voyaging to Troy?
And then the way he broke out with a sore
And was marooned on the commander's orders?
Let me tell you, son, the way they abandoned me.
The sea and the sea-swell had me all worn out,
So I dozed and fell asleep under a rock
Down on the shore.
                    And there and then, just like that,

They headed off.
                         And they were delighted.
                                          And the only thing
They left me was a bundle of old rags.
Some day I want them all to waken up
The way I did that day. Imagine, son.
The bay all empty. The ships all disappeared.
Absolute loneliness. Nothing there except
The beat of the waves and the beat of my raw wound.

But I had to keep alive. Crawling and twisting
To get myself down for a drink of water.
Think of what that was like in the wintertime,
When the water got iced over. And then I'd have to
Gather sticks and break them,
                                    and every day
Start a fire from scratch, out of two flints.
Terrible times.
                         I managed to come through
But I never healed.
                         My whole life has been
Just one long cruel parody.

This island is a nowhere. Nobody
Would ever put in here. There's nothing.
Nothing to attract a lookout's eye.
Nobody in his right mind would come near it.
And the rare ones that ever did turn up
Landed by accident, against their will.
They would take pity on me, naturally.
Share out their supplies and give me clothes.
But not a one of them would ever, ever
Take me on board with them to ship me home.

Every day has been a weeping wound
For ten years now. Ten years' misery and starvation –
That's all my service ever got for me.
That's what I have to thank Odysseus for
And Menelaus and Agamemnon.

                              Gods curse them all!
I ask for the retribution I deserve.
I solemnly beseech the gods to strike
The sons of Atreus in retaliation.

CHORUS
I know the way those people must have felt
When they landed here and saw you.

NEOPTOLEMUS
And I know from experience, Philoctetes,
That this has the ring of truth. I know
What Odysseus and that whole crowd are like.

PHILOCTETES
                              How is that?
Have you a score to settle with them too?

NEOPTOLEMUS
I'll choke them all some day with my two bare hands
And let them know that Scyros is a match
For Sparta and Mycenae put together.

PHILOCTETES
More power to you, child!
                    But what brought you here
If you're so desperate to be after them?

NEOPTOLEMUS

I'll tell you – though you of all men know
What it's like when you've been humiliated.
Still, humiliate me was what they did.
After my father died, there came a day . . .

PHILOCTETES

Achilles died?
　　　　　Achilles?
　　　　　　　　　How? What happened?

NEOPTOLEMUS

Human enemies did not slay Achilles.
It was the great god Apollo.

PHILOCTETES

No shame, in that event, on either side . . .
Your father, dead. I'm heartbroken for him.

NEOPTOLEMUS

You have heartbreak enough, Philoctetes,
Without starting to take on another man's.

PHILOCTETES

You're right.
　　　　　You are right.
　　　　　　　　　So keep on with the story.

NEOPTOLEMUS

My father's foster-father and Odysseus
Landed from Troy in a freshly rigged-out boat.
They had crucial information, they maintained,
And to this day I cannot be sure

If it was lies or the truth.
                              What they said
Was this:
                    With Achilles gone,
I was the destined one, the only man
Who could ever take the citadel of Troy.
So, naturally, I went straight into action.
There was the Greek cause, and –

                              inevitably –
There was my father.
                         I wanted to see
My father's body before they buried him.
And behind all that, maybe there was the lure
Of being the one who would take the citadel.

Well. After two days' good sailing,
We disembarked on the shore at Sigeum
And it was a great moment.
                              The whole army
Gathered to salute me, everybody declared
It was just like seeing Achilles in the flesh,
Alive again.
               But Achilles was a corpse.
I mourned him. I took my last look at him
And then went to the sons of Atreus
As friends of mine, for how could they not be?
I made the formal claim for my father's armour
And whatever else was due to me. But they
Violated every law and custom
And said, yes, I could have the personal effects,
But Achilles' arms were being worn already
By another man. By Laertes' son, in fact,
Odysseus himself. And that put me wild.

I raved and cried, then I asked them simply, why?
Why were the weapons not reserved for me?
So who pipes up but Odysseus himself
And says because he was present on the spot
And saved the arms and saved my father's body,
He was entitled.
                    And that put me wilder still.
I had a fit. I savaged him to his face
And insulted him and cursed him. But he comes up –
Not out of control, but definitely provoked –
And he says to me,
                    'We bore the brunt, not you.
When you should have been with us, you went missing.
So rant and rave your fill, but you will never
Be seen in your famous armour on Scyros Island.'

That was enough. There was nothing else to do
But turn round for home, humiliated
By the lowest of the low.
                    But Odysseus
In the end is less responsible
Than the ones who held command.
People in high office are bound to rule
By the force of their example. Bad actions come
From being badly influenced. What you see
Is what you do yourself.
                    Anyway.
That's all I have to say. But you'll understand
Why I consider anyone a friend
That suffered at the hands of that alliance.

CHORUS
I asked the ground to open under them,

22

Menelaus and Agamemnon,
When they demeaned this man.

They robbed him of his father's arms. But worse:
They robbed him of dignity. He lost face.
He was openly insulted by Odysseus.

I asked Earth herself, the mother of Zeus,
The mistress of the bull-killing lions,
Native of gold Pactolus, spirit of mountains.

PHILOCTETES

Well, there's nothing I can teach you
You don't know already. Odysseus
Is contemptible and plausible and dangerous.
And always was. But what about Ajax?
I am astonished Ajax made no moves.
Did he take no hand at all?

NEOPTOLEMUS

Ajax, friend, had died before this started.
If he had been alive, the arms were mine.

PHILOCTETES

Say that again, child. Ajax is dead and gone?

NEOPTOLEMUS

Ajax has gone away out of the light.

PHILOCTETES

And the ones that never should have seen the light
Are thriving still.

NEOPTOLEMUS
They are.
The whole seed, breed and generation of them.
The biggest names in the Greek army now.

PHILOCTETES
But there was one good influence. One good man.
Nestor. My friend, old Nestor of Pylius.
What has become of him?

NEOPTOLEMUS
He's losing ground.
His son, Antilochus, was a casualty
And that weakened Nestor's own position.

PHILOCTETES
This is terrible news. Of all people,
Those two are the last I'd want to think of
Being dead. But they are the ones, of course.
And the one man that does deserve to die –
Odysseus – Odysseus walks free.

NEOPTOLEMUS
Odysseus can outfox most opposition.
But long runs the fox that isn't caught at last.

PHILOCTETES
Gods! I forgot! Patroclus. Where was Patroclus
When you needed him? Where was your father's friend?

NEOPTOLEMUS
Philoctetes. Let me educate you

In one short sentence. War has an appetite
For human goodness but it won't touch the bad.

PHILOCTETES

I'm not going to contradict you there. No,
                              But there was a certain
Gifted, sharp-tongued, useless nobody –

NEOPTOLEMUS

You mean Odysseus?

PHILOCTETES

                    No. Not him.
But a man you couldn't bear to listen to
And therefore the man you had to listen to
Incessantly. I mean Thersites.

NEOPTOLEMUS

I didn't see him. But I know he's still alive.

PHILOCTETES

Of course. Of course. What else could you expect?
The gods do grant immunity, you see,
To everybody except the true and the just.
The more of a plague you are, and the crueller,
The better your chances of being turned away
From the doors of death. Whose side are gods on?
What are human beings to make of them?
How am I to keep on praising gods
If they keep disappointing me, and never
Match the good on my side with their good?

NEOPTOLEMUS

One thing's certain in all this. I intend
To get very far away from that crew camped at Troy.
Once sharks and tramps start being in charge,
All ordinary decency is gone.
In future, the rocks and backwardness
Of my old home will mean far more to me . . .
Which is why I'm bound for Scyros. I have to go
Back down to the ship now. I am sorry,
Philoctetes, but I must say goodbye.
I hope the gods relent and your sores get cured.
We have to head on. Goodbye again, my friend.

PHILOCTETES

Are you going away again as soon as this?

NEOPTOLEMUS

We are. The minute the weather's right.
We have to be standing by for speedy boarding.

PHILOCTETES

No. Wait, son. Listen. And when I ask
What I am asking of you now, remember
Your own father and mother.
You know how your heart lifts when you think of home?
Well, think of what it's like to be me here,
Always homesick, abandoned every time.
Take me with you. As a passenger.
The state I'm in, I know I'm the last thing
A crew would want on board. But, do it, son,
Even so. Make yourself go through with it.
Generous people should follow their instincts.
Saying no is not your natural way

And even if you do, you'll suffer for it.
So go with your impulse, take me to Oeta,
And you'll be proud, and people will be proud
Of you.
        You could do it all in a day.
One single day. You can stow me anywhere.
The hold. The stern. Up under the prow.
Wherever I'm the least bother to the men.
Come on now, son. It's in you to do this.
You're not going to leave a wounded man behind.
I'm on my knees to you, look, and me not fit
To move hardly. I'm lamed for life. I'm done.

Take me out of here. Take me home with you
To your place, or somewhere in Euboea.
It'll be easy from there to get to Oeta,
And the Trachinian Hills and the Sperchius,
The River Sperchius, flowing away there still.
And my father too.
           So long ago, my father.
But I am afraid, not any more.
             Time
After time, when they would sail away,
I would send word. But my predicament
Was the last thing on their minds. So probably
He never got my news. Or else he's dead.
But you'll take my message this time, and take me
As well.
        Life is shaky. Never, son, forget
How risky and slippy things are in this world.
Walk easy when the jug's full, and don't ever
Take your luck for granted. Count your blessings
And always be ready to pity other people.

Pity him, sir, do.
The man's at breaking point.
Imagine he was your friend.
And you didn't take him then?
It would cry out to heaven.

You have it in for the sons of Atreus,
So now's your chance to thwart them.
Take Philoctetes home
In your speedy ship. Do justice
And upset them – all at once.

NEOPTOLEMUS

Be sure this just isn't all loose talk.
Take care that you aren't going to change your tune
When he's stinking up the boat, and your stomach's
    turning.

CHORUS

Trust us. We're not going to renege.

NEOPTOLEMUS

If that's the case, then, I'll not have it said
I ever stopped a stranger being helped.
                        But we have to get a move on.
He's welcome, he's in with us, so get him ready
And we'll be off, to wherever the gods grant
Safe passage and plain sailing.

PHILOCTETES

This is a happy day! And you, son dear,
And all of you, how will I ever manage

To pay you back? Friends! Friends,
We have to go, but before we go, I want
To kiss this ground . . . Take one last farewell
Of a home where I never was at home.
You have to realize the way I lived.
Many's another would have given up.
For most people, one glimpse of the life here
Would have been enough. But I was fit for it.
I matched necessity. I passed the test.

CHORUS

Hold on a moment. There are two people here.
The one from the ship I recognize, but not
The other one. We should see what they want.

Enter MERCHANT *(in disguise).*

MERCHANT

Son of Achilles, I was told of your whereabouts
By the watchman at the boat.

                    Lucky for you
That we landed here at all, in fact.

                        Pure chance.
Anyhow, I'm a skipper with a fleet
Of merchant vessels, coming back from Troy.
And when I heard from your sailors you were captain
I thought the right thing was to get in touch
Before I sailed – for your own good, that is,
And maybe do myself a good turn too.

                        Who knows?
Let me just say, then:
There are certain things you should be aware of.

The Greeks have plans for you, and some of them
Are going ahead already as we speak.

NEOPTOLEMUS
A good deed should be rewarded, friend,
So you'll be treated right. I'll see to that.
But what's your news exactly? What are these moves?

MERCHANT
Old Phoenix and two sons of Theseus
Are on the high seas after you.

NEOPTOLEMUS
Why this time? To snatch me or negotiate?

MERCHANT
I've no idea. I'm telling you all I know.

NEOPTOLEMUS
But why are Phoenix and those two young fellows
In such a hurry to please the leadership?

MERCHANT
This is it . . . But you have to realize
This is what you are actually up against.

NEOPTOLEMUS
And why not Odysseus this time too?
Was he too scared to volunteer? I can't believe it!

MERCHANT
Odysseus? Oh, he was gone already

When I set sail. He and Tydeus' son
Were away after another, different man.

NEOPTOLEMUS
So what about this other man? What sent
Odysseus after him? Who is he?

MERCHANT
Oh! He's himself, somewhere . . .

But you tell me,
And keep your voice down when you do: who's this?

NEOPTOLEMUS
This, friend, is the famous Philoctetes.

MERCHANT
That's that, then. End of questions. Time to go.
Get yourself on board and get as far
Away from this island as you ever can.

PHILOCTETES
What's he saying there? What bad is this man
Trying to put into your head about me?

NEOPTOLEMUS
I can make no sense of it myself. But
Whatever it is, he'll have to speak it out,
In the open, to you, to me, and everyone.

MERCHANT
Son of Achilles, don't report me. Don't
Get me into trouble with the army.

I'm only a trader and have to trade
In whatever's going. Like information.

NEOPTOLEMUS

Look. This man and I are two fast friends.
Both of us have our knife in that Atreus clan.
But you have come to me as a friend as well,
So keep nothing back, from me *or* from him.

MERCHANT

Well. For your own good, you should watch yourself.

NEOPTOLEMUS

I can watch myself.

MERCHANT

All right, then.
Here is the story as I understand it.
Odysseus and the other captain sailed
In pursuit of Philoctetes here.
They have sworn to take him into custody
One way or another. If they can't
Manage to soft-soap him, they'll use force.
Odysseus declared all this in public.
He was far more overbearing than the other.

NEOPTOLEMUS

But they did their dirty work on Philoctetes
Years ago, so what's possessed them now?
Why do they all of a sudden want him back?
Fear of the gods? Remorse? I wouldn't think it.

I can see I have to start at the beginning
And get this whole thing clear, once and for all.

                                        All right.
First, you should know about a soothsayer
Called Helenus.

                    A Trojan.

                                One of Priam's sons.
So Odysseus organizes a night raid
And with all his usual old dirty dodges
He captures this Helenus and shows him off
In front of the Greek army. But Helenus
Can more than hold his own. He prophesies
And the gist of his prophecy concerns
This man.

                                He tells the Greeks
That unless they can coax Philoctetes
To leave this island – of his own accord –
They are never going to take the town of Troy.

Well, that was what got Odysseus interested.
His line was simple: he would bring Philoctetes
And make a show of him among the ranks.
If he came willingly, then well and good.
If not, no matter. He would still be forced to come.
And Odysseus makes a vow of this and says,
'You can take the head off me,' he says,
'Cut off my head,

                    if I don't deliver Philoctetes.'
So, young man. That's it. And if you have sense,
You'll mind yourself – whatever about him –
And make tracks out of here.

PHILOCTETES

                    Oh! Desperate! Desperate!
Incredible that he could even imagine it,
Think that he could ever talk me back among them.
There's about as much chance of that as of me
Rising from the dead.

MERCHANT

              Well, whatever.
I'm away back now to the ship.

                              The pair of you
Are in the lap of the gods.

                        I wish you well.

Exit MERCHANT.

PHILOCTETES

Can you believe this, child? Odysseus
Thinks it possible he can cajole me
Into a ship, and back to face the Greeks.
I'd sooner meet the snake that poisoned me.
I'd sooner its forked tongue any day than his.
He has the neck for anything, nothing
Is sacrosanct, he'll say and do the worst.
I know him, and I know he will be here.

                              So, set sail.
Get as much ocean as you can between
Him and us. It's action stations now!

NEOPTOLEMUS

We need the wind behind us. We can't move
Till it changes in our favour.

34

PHILOCTETES

Everything has to favour any move
Out of harm's way.

NEOPTOLEMUS

        True enough.
But what's against us is also against them.

PHILOCTETES

It'll be for them, one way or another.
You can never blow a pirate off his course.

NEOPTOLEMUS

All right. We will go now. But first, think:
Is there anything here you really need?

PHILOCTETES

                Only one thing.
Not much, but still essential.

NEOPTOLEMUS

Something we wouldn't have on board the ship?

PHILOCTETES

I've got this store of herbs put by, for when
The sore gets bad. They ease the pain a bit.

NEOPTOLEMUS

Bring them with you, then, and whatever else.

PHILOCTETES

The only other thing would be the arrows
I might have dropped.

Nobody else must ever
Lay hands on them.

NEOPTOLEMUS
And that, in your hands there:
Is that the bow?

PHILOCTETES
This is the bow.
I inherited this from Hercules
When his body burned on the funeral pyre
And his name became a god's.

NEOPTOLEMUS
The bow
Is like a god itself.
I feel this urge
To touch it.
For its virtue.
Venerate it.
Can I hold it in my hands?

PHILOCTETES
If you can't hold it, child,
Then who else can? From now on, what's mine is yours.

NEOPTOLEMUS
I want to take it but I don't want to
Go beyond the bounds of what is allowed.

PHILOCTETES
You are allowed, son. Your natural reverence
Gives you the right. You've brought back sunlight here.

You've lit the world and now I'm fit to see
A way home to my father and my friends.
I was under the heel of enemies
But you raised me up above them.
You of all men have the right to hold
Philoctetes' bow. What's mine is yours.
You gave to me, I give to you . . .

(The bow is proffered, elevated and held significantly between them.)

You and you alone can tell the world
You touched this weapon, and the reason why
Is the reason I got it from Hercules
In the first place: generous behaviour.

NEOPTOLEMUS
There's a whole economy of kindness
Possible in the world; befriend a friend
And the chance of it's increased and multiplied.
Come on now. Check the cave.

PHILOCTETES
                                        But you come too.
I am hardly fit.

Exit PHILOCTETES *and* NEOPTOLEMUS *up to cave.*

CHORUS
You've heard the famous tale
Of Ixion on his wheel:
When he wanted Zeus's wife
Zeus punished him for life
And bent him like a hoop.

Ixion courted fate
And had to suffer for it.
But Philoctetes, no.
He didn't seduce or kill.
He was just and dutiful.

Think what that man came through.
What did he ever do
To be cursed with his abscess,
Crippled and deserted,
Doomed in a wilderness?

When he could bear no more,
The pain kept on. His sore
Made him squeal and scream
For somebody to come.
But nobody ever came.

He crept round like an infant.
He wept. And when he hunted
For herbs to soothe the foot,
The foot wept as he dragged it.
His trail was blood and matter.

But when an infant creeps
And hurts himself and weeps,
The helping hand is there.
For Philoctetes, never:
His echo was his neighbour.

No cultivated ground,
No field where crops abound,
No milled grain or bread.

Only what he could kill
With his great bowman's skill.

But now it is farewell
To the thicket and the pool.
Now it's wine in the bowl.
Set out in his father's house –
To give thanks and to bless.

With Neoptolemus
He will voyage to where
He knows each well and river,
And Hercules's pyre
Blazed once upon the hills.

NEOPTOLEMUS *and* PHILOCTETES *come out of the cave.* NEOP-
TOLEMUS *gets down to a lower level.* PHILOCTETES *arrested
higher up, gradually rocking a little and supported on the bow.*

NEOPTOLEMUS

All right.
     We'd better go.
          What's wrong with you?

PHILOCTETES

Ahhhhhhhhh. Ahhhhhhhhh. Hohohohohoh.

NEOPTOLEMUS

What is this anyway?

PHILOCTETES

Nothing.
     Nothing's wrong.
          You keep going.

NEOPTOLEMUS
Is it the ulcer? Is it going to start?

PHILOCTETES
I don't think so.
          No harm.
                    You keep going.
O gods! O holy gods! Oh! Ohhhhh! Ohhhhhhh!

NEOPTOLEMUS
What are we going to do? You're in awful pain.

PHILOCTETES
This is the end, son.
                This ruins everything.
I'm being cut open! Can you not do anything?
It's coming now. It's coming.
                   Oh! Ah! AHHHHHHH!
Get your sword, son. Take the sword to me.
Cut off that foot.
            Destroy it.
                    Give me peace.
Quick, quick, quick, do something!
                       I want to die.

A silence.

NEOPTOLEMUS
Philoctetes. What has come over you?
What is this turn? Can you still hear me?

PHILOCTETES
You know . . .

NEOPTOLEMUS
Know what?

PHILOCTETES
                    All these spasms of mine . . .

NEOPTOLEMUS
What about them?

PHILOCTETES
I can't go on. I'm done.

NEOPTOLEMUS
You were at the limit. At the breaking point.

PHILOCTETES
There are no words for it. Only pity.
                                        Pity.

NEOPTOLEMUS
But what am I going to do?

PHILOCTETES
Whatever you do, don't leave. Don't let me
Scare you.
            This thing comes over me.
                                    One minute
It's nowhere and the next I'm squalling.

NEOPTOLEMUS
This is terrible. There must be something
I could do. Can I not give you a hand?
Would it not help you just to hold on to me?

41

PHILOCTETES

No! No! Don't touch me. But you can hold the bow.
You'll have to guard it till this turn is over.
The pain will run its course, and once it eases
I'll go straight to sleep. Out like a light.
That'll mean I'm on the mend, so let me sleep.
But if any of them land when I'm like that,
I bind you in the sight of all the gods:
Never part with this bow. Willingly
Or unwillingly. That will be fatal. Fatal
For you, and for me that's in your power.
Do you understand?

NEOPTOLEMUS

        Easy, Philoctetes. Rely on me.
No other hands will ever touch this bow
But yours and mine. Trust fate. Give it over.

PHILOCTETES

Here is the bow for you. Here are the arrows.
Dangerous weapons. And dangerous because
They tempt the gods to be jealous of your luck.
So say a prayer that you'll come through this better
Than I did, and the man that gave them to me.

NEOPTOLEMUS

I will pray for that.
        But I also pray
That the gods' intentions and our destination
Won't be at odds, and they speed us on our journey.

PHILOCTETES

O son, take care I am not a stumbling block

To this prayer of yours. I'm all blood again.
I'm open deeper than ever. It's pouring out.
It's here again. Circling for a kill.
Why me? Gods curse this foot.

                              Oh. Ahhhhhh.
No, wait. Don't go. Don't let me scare you.
Shout instead. Shout hard. Shout their names.
Odysseus. Agamemnon. Menelaus.
I'll be the death of them. Let me smit them all.
O son, my body's burning.
                        Could you not
Carry me up to the crater of Lemnos
And burn me right?
                    What I did for Hercules
You should do for me.
                        Throw me into the fire
And keep the bow.
                    Are you there, son?
                                Say something.
Where are you?

NEOPTOLEMUS
I'm here. I'm here.
                        But I'm useless.
I know it's desperate.

PHILOCTETES
As long as you are there, that does me good.
And it's going to go soon, all of a sudden,
Just the way it came.

43

NEOPTOLEMUS
We're staying with you.
Don't worry about that.

PHILOCTETES
You're going to stay?

NEOPTOLEMUS
I promise.

PHILOCTETES
Promise. What use is promise?
Swear it to me.
But no. Swear nothing.
Son,
I am astray. What am I saying?

NEOPTOLEMUS
I tell you, Philoctetes, I am bound
To you, and bound to take you.

PHILOCTETES
So. Give me your hand.

NEOPTOLEMUS
Gladly. Here. We are well and truly pledged.

PHILOCTETES
Good. Good. Now the way is open.

NEOPTOLEMUS
What way? Where?

44

PHILOCTETES

Up there. Into the sky world. High beyond.

NEOPTOLEMUS

He's raving now again. What do you see?

PHILOCTETES

Let me go. Don't touch me. Stay away!

NEOPTOLEMUS

I will. But you stay calm.
                              That's right. Stretch out.

PHILOCTETES

From now on, I am going to belong
Entirely to the earth. Be earth's for the taking.
I'll lie on top here first, and then lie under.

NEOPTOLEMUS

This man's bound to sleep now, very soon.
He's sweated out, the head is down, and his whole
Body is exhausted.
                    The flux has stopped,
There's hardly any issue from his foot.
We should leave him quiet, friends, to get some rest.

(*If there is to be an interval, it occurs now.*)

CHORUS

Sleep is the god-sent cure.
Deep-reaching, painless, sure.
Its touch is certain.
The light of paradise

Creeps into sleepers' eyes
As through a curtain.

But you, sir, must wake up.
Don't let this moment slip.
Hold off no longer.
Now that the coast is clear
You have to do and dare.
You were never stronger.

Obviously now we could steal away with the bow.
That would be easy. But easy and meaningless. No.
It's to this wounded man the triumph has to be due.
He has earned it. The oracle said it. I see it all now.
Without him the cause will be shamed and our victory
    hollow.

Oracles are devious,
Beyond the likes of us.
We don't inquire too deep.
And we keep our voices down,
For sick men have been known
To hear things in their sleep.

Take care. Chances like this
You can't afford to miss.
Even a fool can see
There's trouble brewing.
So move. Immediately.

The man is at death's door.
You couldn't ask for more.
The winds are for us.
Before the birds can scare
Wise huntsmen draw the snare
And the noose closes.

NEOPTOLEMUS

Quiet. This is nonsense. Give it over.
There's a flicker in the eyes there. His head's moving.

PHILOCTETES

The light.
  Sunlight.
    And you still here, my friends.
I never thought I'd waken up like this.
I never thought you'd stand your ground with me.
I didn't think you'd have the heart for it.
It was different, I tell you, the first time here.
But, Neoptolemus, you are no betrayer.
You're no Odysseus, and couldn't be.
You have it in you from both sides, straight and true
By nature. You made light of everything,
The reeks and roars and the whole mess of me.
But that's all over now. So, help me up.
Put me on my feet here. Stand me straight
And once I'm steadied right, then everybody
Can go down to the boat, and all set sail.

NEOPTOLEMUS

This is more than I expected. It's great
You've come round again, that you're alive
And out of danger.

47

Up you get!
Or if you'd rather, we could carry you.
These men are fit for that. Whatever you like.

PHILOCTETES

That's a real friend's thought. And since you thought it,
Lift me, you yourself. Don't bother them.
They'll all be sickened of me soon enough
Once we're on board.

NEOPTOLEMUS

So. On your feet, then.
Get yourself together.

PHILOCTETES

All right. All right.
I'll be
Into my stride in no time.

NEOPTOLEMUS

What's to become of me now anyway?

PHILOCTETES

What's to become of who?
What is it, child?

NEOPTOLEMUS

I'm all throughother.
This isn't me.
I'm sorry.

PHILOCTETES

What has upset you now? Don't be afflicted.

NEOPTOLEMUS

I'm an affliction to myself, that's all I am.

PHILOCTETES

Have you changed your mind? Can you not face the
    thing?
Does having to ship with me disgust you that much?

NEOPTOLEMUS

It's more like self-disgust. No. One false move,
One move that's not your own, and everything
Goes to the bad.

PHILOCTETES

                        This is not you. Who, son,
Was ever more like himself or them before him?

NEOPTOLEMUS

I'll be seen for what I am.
                                    I just can't face it.

PHILOCTETES

Face what? What false move? What do you mean?

NEOPTOLEMUS

Zeus, you must help me now. There's no way out.
If I tell or if I don't tell, it's still disgrace.

PHILOCTETES

Unless I'm wrong, I think – but no – not him –
I think that he's for sailing on without me!

NEOPTOLEMUS

Oh no. I won't be leaving you. And more's the pity.
We'll both rue that.

PHILOCTETES

There's no sense in this.

NEOPTOLEMUS

There is sense in it all right, Philoctetes.
The real story is this: you will be sailing,
Sailing to Troy to connect up with the Greeks.

PHILOCTETES

What?
       What?
              What sort of talk is this?

NEOPTOLEMUS

Quiet. Hold on. Listen.
                        There's a meaning to it.

PHILOCTETES

Meaning? What meaning? How could there be meaning?

NEOPTOLEMUS

I have to take you from this plight you're in.
You have to go with me and level Troy.

PHILOCTETES

Never.
       Never.
              That will never happen.

None of us can dictate the shape of things.
It's all laid out. I'm not the one to blame.

PHILOCTETES
You're as two-faced as the rest. Why did you do it?
Who are you?
                    Give me back my bow.

NEOPTOLEMUS
I cannot.
          There's a cause, a plan, big moves,
And I'm a part of them. I'm under orders.

PHILOCTETES
Burnt bones!
          Sears and blisters!
                              There was more left
Of Hercules on the pyre than's left of me.
The salamanders have me. I'm scorched to nothing.

I kneeled to him. How can he bear to do it?
Steal the bow and leave me as good as dead?
And still not say a word. Not meet my eye.
Hard little two-faced crab. He knows. He knows
He's reneging on doing the right thing.

What will I do? What's left here now but me
And the place itself? The island's all there is
That'll stand to me. If I turn and leave,
The cliffs and caves and bays will still be there
When I come back. If I shout for sympathy
To animals and birds, they'll answer me.

51

There's more nature in their dens and nests
Than there is in you, you sacrilegious
Heartbreaking little coward.
                              But the man you tricked
Was never the man you came to snatch away.
You'll be showing off a phantom to the Greeks
And your big name and fame will always be
Hollow to the core.
                    You faced nothing here.
You overpowered a cripple without weapons,
And even then, you did it underhand.

O son, be yourself again. This isn't you.
Give me the bow.
                              Still nothing.
He's condemning me to a death by hunger.
I'm going to be a ghost before my time.
                              The birds and brutes
I slaughtered with the bow, they're closing in.
I can see their beaks and muzzles crowding up
Both ends of the cave. They'll pick me clean.
My life for theirs, eye and tooth and claw.
                              Look at him there!
Any kind of trust is a mistake!

Oh, but, son, you don't want to believe
That's how it is. Change things back again
And change your mind. My tongue could hardly bear
To curse you after all I felt for you.

Why are we listening to this now, sir? Are we
On our way or not? What are you thinking?

NEOPTOLEMUS

I can't help it. There's something in me he touched
From the very start. I can't just cut him off.

PHILOCTETES

The gods have their eyes on him and that's why
He can't get off the hook. He knows all this
Solidarity with the Greeks is sham.
The only real thing is the thing he lives for:
                                 his own self-respect.

NEOPTOLEMUS

How did I end up here? Why did I go
Behind backs ever?

PHILOCTETES

                 You did it because
You had agreed to do it. Somebody else
Rehearsed you. It has to be. There's nothing low
Or crooked in you at all. Come on, child.
Give me the bow.

NEOPTOLEMUS

                 Well, friends, where are we now?

NEOPTOLEMUS *moves,* PHILOCTETES *reaches, the body
language and handling of the bow suggest that their original
mutual rite of exchange will now be repeated. It is a slightly
somnambulant movement, which* ODYSSEUS *interrupts, coming
between them suddenly, his back to* PHILOCTETES.

ODYSSEUS

Now who's the bow for, Neoptolemus?

Hand it over! A traitor can't expect
To carry weapons.

PHILOCTETES
Odysseus! That voice!
It has to be.

ODYSSEUS
Odysseus
That was and is!

PHILOCTETES
And when else but now?
Hangmen and betrayers never show
Till the moment's ripe.

ODYSSEUS
That I don't deny.

PHILOCTETES
Return my bow, now, boy. You nearly did.

ODYSSEUS
He nearly did but now he never will,
And you have your marching orders. Understand:
The bow goes, and you with it, with these men.

PHILOCTETES
Are you going to herd me like a wild animal?

ODYSSEUS
That's up to you. Everybody else
Wants you to come back of your own free will.

PHILOCTETES

Ground of my island, be with me here and now.
And Vulcan, lord of forge-fire, volcano god,
Scorch the earth and brand the hills of Lemnos
With the mark of my ordeal at his hands.

ODYSSEUS

My hands, Philoctetes, are in the hands
Of Zeus. Zeus and his thunderbolts
Rule Vulcan even. Zeus is the Lord of Lemnos.

PHILOCTETES

Anything that comes out of your mouth
Just turns to dirt. Don't foul the name of Zeus.
No god could stoop as low as Odysseus.

ODYSSEUS

What do gods care? It's what they say that matters
And they say you'll march.

PHILOCTETES

          I say not.

ODYSSEUS

Say what you like, but you'll obey and move.

PHILOCTETES

Like a slave in chains. Oh, weep for the free man
That's broken here.

ODYSSEUS

         No. Wrong. The free man here
Is being raised up. These are his first steps
Towards Troy and triumph.

Never. Not while earth
Is under me and the rocks above.

What blather's this?

I can throw myself
From any cliff or headland on this island.

There! Get him by the arms. He's asking for it.

Odysseus, you have taken everything I ever had and
was. The best years of my life, my means of self-
defence, my freedom, the use of my two hands.
Everything that made me my own self, you've
stripped away. And now you're going to take my
second self. This boy. He's your accomplice but he
was my friend. With you he does what he is told, with
me he did what his nature told him. I made him free,
you only fouled him up. Look at him there, he can't
look me in the eye, he knows he's contaminated. My
body may be corrupting but with him it is the mind,
and you did that. You spread death-in-life. I am like
a lost soul bound for Hades, being led away out of
the house of life and light and friendship.

I curse you. I have cursed you always. It changes
nothing. I'm chaff and you're the flail. I'm beaten to
nothing. I'm gone out of mind now like a man that's
dead.

So why, why are you tearing me up out of the
grave? Has the bad smell left me? Will you not start
vomiting all over the altar now again? Will I not make
you get sick into the holy vessels this time? That was
your excuse, don't you forget. That was why you
dumped me.

But the wheel is turning, the scales are tilting back.
Justice is going to waken up at last. The gods were
only biding time and the time has gone. It wasn't love
of me that brought you to this island, there's a shape
to this that's bigger than you could know. Your eye's
so jaundiced, you can't see the balance shifting and
weighing down against you – but I see it and my heart
is singing. I'd give the whole agony of my life just to
see you cut down in the end, and your tongue ripped
out of you like a bleeding ox-tongue.

CHORUS
This is terrible talk. I always heard
Suffering made people compassionate,
But it's only made him harder.

ODYSSEUS
                    There's plenty
I could tell him, and tell about him,
If there was time. But I'll say only this:
My aim has always been to get things done
By being adaptable. If I'm dealing with
Plain-spoken, honest people, they'll find me
As honest and plain-spoken as they come.
My main concern is to keep things moving on
In the right direction.
                    But in this case, no.

57

Not any more.
              I give up.
                       Let him go.
He's welcome to his island. All we need
Is Philoctetes' bow. Not him. Don't forget
I am the bender of as great a bow
Myself. And don't forget Teucer either.
You're only another archer among archers.
And since you're so worried about who's going to be
The Lord of Lemnos, you be it yourself.
You should have been the Lord of Fallen Troy
But that's an honour fallen now to me.

PHILOCTETES

You of all of them!

ODYSSEUS
               Enough said. Time to move!

PHILOCTETES

Son of Achilles, are you going to go
Without one word still? Don't deny yourself.

ODYSSEUS

Ignore him, Neoptolemus. The thing's
Ruined if you start shilly-shallying.

PHILOCTETES

And what about the rest of you?
Where's your pity now? Are you all just yes-men?

CHORUS

When the captain speaks, the crew has to obey.

NEOPTOLEMUS
Whether it's shilly-shallying or not,
What you'll do is wait here to the last
When all the prayers and thanksgivings are over
And the boat's rigged out.

                    Maybe he'll come round
And see the sense of moving with us yet.
I'm away on with Odysseus.

                         You hear?
Be ready and be listening for the shout.

Exit ODYSSEUS *and* NEOPTOLEMUS.

PHILOCTETES
I am going to die here,
I'm going to die of hunger,
That's what's going to happen.
Trapped among fallen rocks
In the bare mouth of a cave.
Watching clouds and birds
Blowing across the sky.
No bow any more.
Slow death by exposure.

CHORUS
You walked yourself into it. Don't protest and lament
As if at this stage your whole predicament
Was unavoidable. It is not Odysseus
But your own self you have to blame for this.

PHILOCTETES
Some animals in a trap
Eat their own legs off

In order to escape.
I'd like to see him caught
And so stuck and smashed up
He couldn't do even that.

We had no hand in whatever scheme he laid,
So listen to us: don't contradict a god.
I sense that there's some overarching fate
You must obey. I say this in all friendship.

He'll be sitting laughing at me,
Sitting watching the sea
Somewhere, him and the bow.
Turning it over and over,
Trying it out in his hands,
Testing the weight and the lift.
I loved the feel of it,
Its grip and give, and the grain
That was seasoned with my sweat.
When I held it, I had a hold
On the crossbeam of the world.
I was the wind and the trees
And the pillar of Hercules.
But now he's sitting with it,
Laughing and turning it over.
                    Great gods, be just!
I am mocked and accursed
And I hate that man for ever.

If you seek justice, you should deal justly always.

60

You should govern your tongue and present a true case.
For don't forget: Odysseus was commanded.
There was nothing personal in what he did.

PHILOCTETES

I'll soon be tainted meat
For scavengers to pick at.
The shining eyes and claws
Of all the hunted creatures
Are sharpening for a kill:
Crows and wolves and vultures
And every animal
That was my victim ever.
I'm at their mercy now.
This is the last stand
And I haven't an arrow even.
All I've left is a wound.

CHORUS

Your wound is what you feed on, Philoctetes.
I say it again in friendship and say this:
Stop eating yourself up with hate and come with us.

PHILOCTETES

I can feel your sympathy,
And did feel it all along.
But now leave me alone.
Once bitten is hard-bitten.
Stop this torturing me.

CHORUS

What torture?

PHILOCTETES
All talk of Troy and me, me
That was stabbed in the back, going back ever.

CHORUS
For your own good you have to.

PHILOCTETES
For my own good,
For the last time, leave me alone!

CHORUS
All right.

All right.
Goodbye.
You are on your own.
We're back to the rowing benches and the rowing.

PHILOCTETES
No. Wait.
Not yet.
Are you away for good?

CHORUS
Easy.
Take it easy.

PHILOCTETES
No! Hold on still!

CHORUS
What's wrong? What is it now?

PHILOCTETES

                                  The foot! The foot!
Being left with that, left on my own again.

CHORUS

                                What do you want?
Are you for coming with us now or are you not?

PHILOCTETES

The sore has me astray. I can't think right.

CHORUS

But listen to yourself.
                        You want to come.

PHILOCTETES

Never. No. No matter how I'm besieged.
I'll be my own Troy. The Greeks will never take me.
But, friends, still, friends, there is one last thing.

CHORUS

                                    What is it?

PHILOCTETES

Have you not a sword for me? Or an axe?
                              Or something?

CHORUS

What for?

PHILOCTETES

What for? What do you think for?
For foot and head and hand. For the relief
Of cutting myself off. I want away.

CHORUS

How away?

PHILOCTETES

Away to the house of death.
To my father, sitting waiting there
Under the clay roof. I'll come back in to him
Out of the light, out of his memory
Of the day I left.

                        We'll be on the riverbank
Again, and see the Greeks arriving
And me setting out for Troy,

                      in all good faith.

CHORUS

Setting-out time is here for us anyhow.
But maybe not.
              There's something holding these two.

Enter NEOPTOLEMUS *and* ODYSSEUS.

ODYSSEUS

What has you so worked up? Why can we not
Just rise and go? What's on your mind?

NEOPTOLEMUS

I did a wrong thing and I have to right it.

ODYSSEUS

What was that?

NEOPTOLEMUS
I did this whole thing your way.

ODYSSEUS
We were Greeks with a job to do, and we did it.

NEOPTOLEMUS
I behaved like a born liar.

ODYSSEUS
But it worked!
It worked, so what about it?

NEOPTOLEMUS
Not for me.
And I'm not leaving till the thing's put right.

ODYSSEUS
It's the bow. You're having second thoughts.

NEOPTOLEMUS
What else?

ODYSSEUS
You mean you're going to just give it back?

NEOPTOLEMUS
The scales will even out when the bow's restored.

ODYSSEUS

Act your age. Be reasonable. Use your head.

NEOPTOLEMUS

Since when did the use of reason rule out truth?

ODYSSEUS

Neoptolemus: am I hearing right?

NEOPTOLEMUS

Oh yes. Loud and clear, and more and more.

ODYSSEUS

I'd have been better then not hearing you.

NEOPTOLEMUS

Too bad. Too late.

ODYSSEUS

Oh, not too late at all.
There's one last barrier you'll not get past.

NEOPTOLEMUS

What's that?

ODYSSEUS

The will of the Greek people,
And me here as their representative.

NEOPTOLEMUS

What kind of talk is that? You're capable,
Odysseus, and resourceful. But you have no values.

ODYSSEUS

And where's the value in your carry-on?

NEOPTOLEMUS

Candour before canniness. Doing the right thing
And not just saying it.

ODYSSEUS

What's so right about
Reneging on your Greek commission?
You're under my command here. Don't you forget it.

NEOPTOLEMUS

The commands that I am hearing overrule
You and all you stand for.

ODYSSEUS

And what about
The Greeks? Have they no jurisdiction left?

NEOPTOLEMUS

The jurisdiction I am under here
Is justice herself. She isn't only Greek.

ODYSSEUS

You've turned yourself into a Trojan, lad,
And that will have consequences.

NEOPTOLEMUS

So let them come.

ODYSSEUS

(*Reaching for his sword*)
Do you see where this hand is now?

NEOPTOLEMUS

Do you see mine?

ODYSSEUS

Right! What I've seen and heard here, I'll report.
You won't get off with this. I'm going back
To outline all the charges.
You were right
When you said you did a wrong thing here.

Exit ODYSSEUS.

NEOPTOLEMUS

Philoctetes!
Philoctetes! Come out here. Where are you?

Enter PHILOCTETES, *at the cave mouth.*

PHILOCTETES

What's all this now?
Have you not done enough
Damage already?

NEOPTOLEMUS

Listen. Listen to me.

PHILOCTETES

I listened to you once and I believed you.
But never again.

NEOPTOLEMUS

Do you deny
The possibility of a change of heart?

PHILOCTETES

Once was enough. You slithered in like this,
All sincerity till you got the bow.

NEOPTOLEMUS

Things are different now. I ask again:
Are you going to stay here saying no for ever
Or do you come in with us?

PHILOCTETES

I'll never join,
So you can save your breath.

NEOPTOLEMUS

That is your last word?

PHILOCTETES

Utterly. No more.

NEOPTOLEMUS

In that case, I give up.
Reluctantly, regretfully, give up.

PHILOCTETES

What sort of a surrender do you want?

How do you think I could believe you ever,
That told me lies and then when I relented
Opened the trapdoor under me? Gods curse you
And the traitors that you're in with.

NEOPTOLEMUS

Curse no more.
I have the bow for you.
Look. Take it.
Here!

PHILOCTETES
Where's the ambush? This I do not believe.

NEOPTOLEMUS
I swear by the name of Zeus, the almighty god.

PHILOCTETES
Swear, oh, you'll swear! It's only words to you.

NEOPTOLEMUS
It is more than words.
Hold your hand out.
Take it.

PHILOCTETES *comes down. Pause and momentary mutual clasp
to recall original pledging. Enter* ODYSSEUS.

ODYSSEUS
As the gods are my witness, as both of you are Greeks,
In my capacity as your commander,
I forbid the handover of this weapon.
Whether Achilles' son wants it or not,

You are under orders, Philoctetes,
To join the force at Troy.

PHILOCTETES

> And you are in range at last.

He aims the bow.

NEOPTOLEMUS

No, Philoctetes, no!

> Hold off. Don't.
>> Don't!

PHILOCTETES

Let go. How dare you, son?

> Let go!

NEOPTOLEMUS

> You can't.

Exit ODYSSEUS.

PHILOCTETES

He was mine for the taking and you saved him. Why?

NEOPTOLEMUS

It would have been the end of both of us.

PHILOCTETES

Commander, he said. One of the big names.
Big talk only, when all was said and done.

71

NEOPTOLEMUS

Forget about him. You have the bow
And my slate's clean again. The air is cleared.

PHILOCTETES

Entirely.

     You are back to your old self,
Your father's son.

NEOPTOLEMUS

It does me good to hear that.

                   It gives me hope
You might credit what I'm going to tell you.
You know it already anyhow. You know
Human beings have to bear up and face
Whatever's meant to be. There's a courage
And dignity in ordinary people
That can be breathtaking. But you're the opposite.
Your courage has gone wild, you're like a brute
That can only foam at the mouth. You aren't
Bearing up, you are bearing down. Anybody
That ever tries to help you just gets savaged.
You're a wounded man in terrible need of healing
But when your friends try, all you do is snarl
Like some animal protecting cubs.
So listen now to me, Philoctetes,
And brand this into your skull.

                  You're a sick man.
The snake-bite at the shrine was from a god,
But the gods send remedies, and they expect
Obedience then as well.

             You are to come
Of your own free will to the town of Troy.

Asclepius, the healer, you remember,
He'll be there with his sons, and they'll cure you.
Then you're to take your bow and go with me
Into the front line and win the city.

All this must come to pass. A soothsayer,
And a Trojan soothsayer at that, has foretold it.
This is the summer of the fall of Troy.
It'll be talked about for ever and you're to be
The hero that was healed and then went on
To heal the wound of the Trojan war itself.

PHILOCTETES
You're making me see things in such brilliant light
I can't bear it. I've been in the afterlife
For ten years now, ten years of being gone
And being forgotten. Even you, my son,
Won't bring me back. The past is bearable,
The past's only a scar, but the future –
Never. Never again can I see myself
Eye to eye with the sons of Atreus.

What's happened to you, son? This makes no sense.
These people defiled your father's memory
And gave his armour to Odysseus.
Why are you arguing a case for them?
Forget them, and remember what you said
You'd do for me. You made a promise
To take me with you when you were going home
To Scyros. And that's what you must do.
Otherwise, you'll be tainted with their guilt
Just by association.

NEOPTOLEMUS
I can see that.
But even so, the signs are that the gods
Want you to go to Troy, and me with you.

PHILOCTETES
How can you bear to take their side like that?

NEOPTOLEMUS
It's not their side.
It's what our fates involve.

PHILOCTETES
This is real turncoat talk. Have you no shame?

NEOPTOLEMUS
What's the shame in working for a good thing?

PHILOCTETES
But good for who? Me or my enemies?

NEOPTOLEMUS
Am I your friend or not?

PHILOCTETES
I thought you were.

NEOPTOLEMUS
Stop just licking your wounds. Start seeing things.

PHILOCTETES
There's danger in all this somewhere. I can sense it.

NEOPTOLEMUS
The danger is you'll break if you don't bend,
So I give up. From now on, you can live
With every consequence of your decision.

PHILOCTETES
Whatever's been laid out, I'm ready for it.
But there's consequence to your own endeavours:
You gave your word – you pledged with your hand
And promised you'd take me home.
                                        So do that now.
Restore your good name. Bury the name of Troy.

NEOPTOLEMUS
I gave my word. I pledged it with my hand.
My life was an open door that started closing
The minute I landed here. But maybe now
It could open back again. So. We go.

PHILOCTETES
                                        We go?

NEOPTOLEMUS
Gather yourself. Come on.

PHILOCTETES
                        I can't believe it.

NEOPTOLEMUS
The Greeks.
            No, wait.
                        The Greeks'll be after us.

75

PHILOCTETES
Forget them. You'll be safe.

NEOPTOLEMUS
But the country won't be.

PHILOCTETES
I'll be in your country.

NEOPTOLEMUS
And what good's that?

PHILOCTETES
Hercules's bow!

NEOPTOLEMUS
The bow. We have it still.

PHILOCTETES
Hercules's bow is miraculous
And will save us every time.

NEOPTOLEMUS
Then so be it.
This time your farewell is farewell for good.

PHILOCTETES *repeats some part of his original rite of departure. Perhaps he raises both arms, perhaps prostrates himself. A silence then, music perhaps also. Then an eerie, soundless (at first) flash and flame; mountain-rumble far off; an air of danger, settling into a kind of threatened, pre-thunder stillness. Darker stage, a kind of purpled twilight.* CHORUS *in spotlight, positioned as at end of prologue.*

Human beings suffer,
They torture one another,
They get hurt and get hard.
No poem or play or song
Can fully right a wrong
Inflicted and endured.

The innocent in gaols
Beat on their bars together.
A hunger-striker's father
Stands in the graveyard dumb.
The police widow in veils
Faints at the funeral home.

History says, *Don't hope
On this side of the grave.*
But then, once in a lifetime
The longed-for tidal wave
Of justice can rise up,
And hope and history rhyme.

So hope for a great sea-change
On the far side of revenge.
Believe that a further shore
Is reachable from here.
Believe in miracles
And cures and healing wells.

Call miracle self-healing:
The utter, self-revealing
Double-take of feeling.
If there's fire on the mountain

Or lightning and storm
And a god speaks from the sky

That means someone is hearing
The outcry and the birth-cry
Of new life at its term.

*The full thunderclap and eruption-effects occur. Then a lingering,
wavering aftermath of half-light. Brilliant spots find*
PHILOCTETES *and* CHORUS.

PHILOCTETES

(*Crying out*)
 Hercules:
    I saw him in the fire.
 Hercules
    was shining in the air.
I heard the voice of Hercules in my head.

CHORUS

(*Ritually clamant, as* HERCULES)
 I have opened the closed road
 Between the living and the dead
 To make the right road clear to you.
 This is the voice of Hercules now.

 Here on earth my labours were
 The stepping-stones to upper air:
 Lives that suffer and come right
 Are backlit by immortal light.

So let my mind light up your mind.
You must see straight and turn around.
You must complete your oath-bound course.
You cannot yet return to Scyros.

Go, Philoctetes, with this boy,
Go and be cured and capture Troy.
Asclepius will make you whole,
Relieve your body and your soul.

Go, with your bow. Conclude the sore
And cruel stalemate of our war.
Win by fair combat. But know to shun
Reprisal killings when that's done.

Then take just spoils and sail at last
Out of the bad dream of your past.
Make sacrifice. Burn spoils to me.
Shoot arrows in my memory.

And, Neoptolemus, you must be
His twin in arms and archery.
Marauding lions on that shore,
Troy's nemesis and last nightmare.

But when the city's being sacked
Preserve the shrines. Show gods respect.
Reverence for the gods survives
Our individual mortal lives.

PHILOCTETES

Something told me this was going to happen.
Something told me the channels were going to open.
It's as if a thing I knew and had forgotten
Came back completely clear. I can see
The cure at Troy. All that you say
Is like a dream to me and I obey.

NEOPTOLEMUS

And so will I.

CHORUS

Then go, immediately.
The winds are blowing and the tides are high.

PHILOCTETES

(*In a sort of daze, on all fours perhaps, or clasping an upright support: knocked out, flattened*)

But I can't believe I'm going. My head's light at the thought of a different ground and a different sky. I'll never get over Lemnos; this island's going to be the keel under me and the ballast inside me. I'm like a fossil that's being carried away, I'm nothing but cave stones and damp walls and an old mush of dead leaves. The sound of waves in draughty passages. A cliff that's wet with spray on a winter's morning. I feel like the sixth sense of the world. I feel I'm a part of what was always meant to happen, and is happening now at last. Come on, my friends.

CHORUS

Now it's high watermark
And floodtide in the heart
And time to go.
The sea-nymphs in the spray
Will be the chorus now.
What's left to say?

Suspect too much sweet talk
But never close your mind.
It was a fortunate wind
That blew me here. I leave
Half-ready to believe
That a crippled trust might walk

And the half-true rhyme is love.